And I
   CLIMBED
And I
   CLIMBED

Published by TROIKA

First published in 2023

Troika Books Ltd,

Well House, Green Lane, Ardleigh, Colchester, Essex, CO7 7PD, UK

www.troikabooks.com

Text copyright © Stephen Lightbown 2023

Illustrations copyright © Shih-Yu Lin 2023

The moral rights of the author and illustrator have been asserted

All rights reserved

A CIP catalogue record for this book is available

from the British Library

ISBN 978-1-912745-29-6

1 3 5 7 9 10 8 6 4 2

Printed in Poland by Totem.com.pl

And I
Climbed
And I
Climbed

Poems by Stephen Lightbown
Illustrated by Shih-Yu Lin

troika

For Bear

Contents

Introduction	8
Broken Back	11
In Hospital	12
Some Days I Hate You	15
Catch Me If You Can	16
It's Hard To Push A Wheelchair With A Tree In Your Finger	18
Weeping Tree	19
Everyone Tells Me What I Can't Do, Apart From Mum	20
A Poem From Mum	23
Bedtime	24
Red Marks	26
What Do You Think At Night Time?	28
Stabilisers	30
My Brother By Ana	32
Biscuits	33
What Was It The Table Said?	34
Climbing	36
Do You Feel Pain?	37

Why Does Everyone Have Something To Say?	38
Writing My Feelings	40
Keep Talking Little One	42
Memory Wheel	44
My Sister's Legs	46
Why Cosmo Is Annoying By Ana	47
Tractor Boy	48
With A Bit Of Practice	49
The First Day	50
Three Haiku	51
Growing	52
A Poem From Nana	54
Choosing Things	56
Brave Boy	58
Biscuits For Dinner	60
Cloudspotting	62
Pushing	63
Ducks	64
Running Away	66
Good Listener	67

Broken Branches	68
My Heart Beats, I Dance	69
Running A Marathon In Custard	72
The Day Is A Bad Dream On Repeat	74
Sleep-Walking	75
A Kenning About My Wheelchair	76
What To Do With A Dying Tree	77
Huff Stop	78
Bleeding Soil	80
Three More Haikus	81
Pushing Bolder	83
The Greatest Day	84
Today I'm A Tree Too	86
Goalkeeper	87
Be Careful With Scissors	88
If Only Trees Could Catch	89
Cosmo	90
Acknowledgements	93
About The Author	94
About The Illustrator	95

Introduction

And I Climbed And I Climbed is a collection of poems that tells the story of Cosmo, an eight year-old boy who has fallen from a tree in his garden and broken his back. After the accident he is left paralysed and uses a wheelchair to move around.

This is a deeply personal collection because, like Cosmo, I also became paralysed after an accident when I was 16. I was sledging in the snow when I lost control of my sledge and hit a tree. Whilst I was a little older than Cosmo is in the book, you will find many of my experiences in these poems and in Cosmo's thoughts and feelings about what he is going through. And of course, I have included a tree, for obvious reasons.

I wanted to write about the experience of becoming a wheelchair user from a child's perspective. To have disability represented in children's poetry and literature is important to me. I wish that, when I was younger, I had seen more people like me in the books I was reading.

I also believe that it is important that poets and writers with lived experiences like mine get to tell their own stories, so that the voices on the page are authentic.

In *And I Climbed And I Climbed*, Cosmo writes poems to the tree that he fell from, as a way of coming to terms with what has happened to him. In some of the poems he is angry and sad, as you would expect him to be. But in others he is happy and excited, as he rediscovers his voice and his capabilities. I hope you enjoy accompanying Cosmo on his journey.

Stephen Lightbown

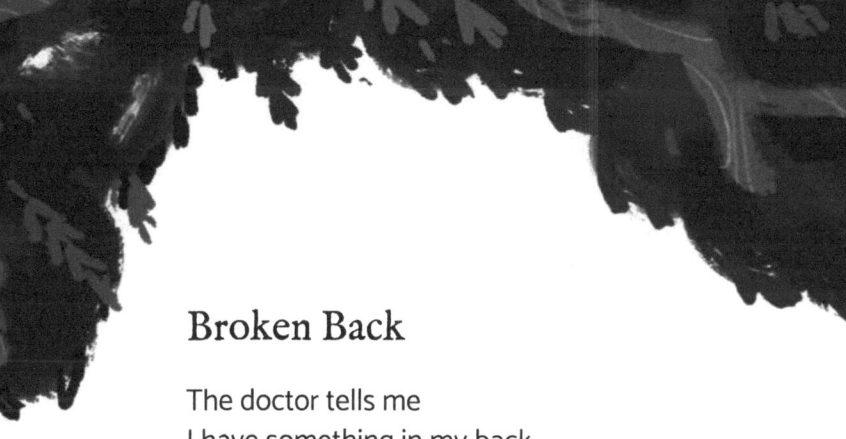

Broken Back

The doctor tells me
I have something in my back
called vertebrae.

He says I have 33.
Is that as many branches
as you have?

I should've tried to count them all
when I climbed through your leaves.

I broke four vertebrae
when I fell from your arms.

Now I use a wheelchair
because, like you,
I can't walk.

In Hospital

On the first day I could eat food, I said I wanted custard.
Not long after, a huge bowl of custard appeared.
On the second and third day I asked for custard.
And it appeared.
I asked how long I could eat custard for.
Until you feel better, they said.

As if you can eat custard every day in a hospital!

After I could manage a full day in my wheelchair
I was told to get ready for Wednesday.
Because on Wednesdays it's swimming.
And when I swim, I feel free. No chair, no pain,
just Cosmo again.

As if they have a swimming pool in a hospital!

The nurse pushed me down to the secret corridor.
The one where they have robots.
Actual robots on wheels–
moving the washing, taking meals, carrying all kinds
 of things I couldn't touch.
These robots are cool, the nurse said.
They're on wheels, just like you. Cool like you.

As if they have robots in a hospital!

After swimming, I ate some toast
and went to look at the robots again.

Some Days I Hate You

and I want the wind to rip you
out of the ground, tear you
from where you feel safe.

Or for someone to take an axe to you,
chop you down till only a stump is left.
Or for your bark to turn rotten
and all your leaves to fall off and never
grow back and you'll stay cold forever.
Or for your tree friends to turn their backs
and leave you alone in the garden.

Then I read that there are three trillion
trees in the world.
I try to count that far, I count up to
one thousand and twenty-six.

That's the furthest I've ever counted.
But then I stop because I count
back to one. You.

And I think out of three trillion
trees, somehow you and I are connected
forever, and I wonder if maybe I should
try to hate you less.

Catch Me If You Can

Sometimes I wonder why you didn't catch me
when I fell through your arms.

My sister Ana – she's five – she looked so small
the higher I climbed. When I got to the top
she looked like I could've put her in my pocket
next to the conkers I'd collected from you.

I climbed
And I climbed
And I climbed
And I climbed

Anna was shouting, begging me to come down.
Her voice
got quieter
        quieter
                quieter

    till all I could hear
was my own breath on your leaves.

I grabbed your branches
and pulled
and pulled
and pulled

till the sky was near
and then I stopped.

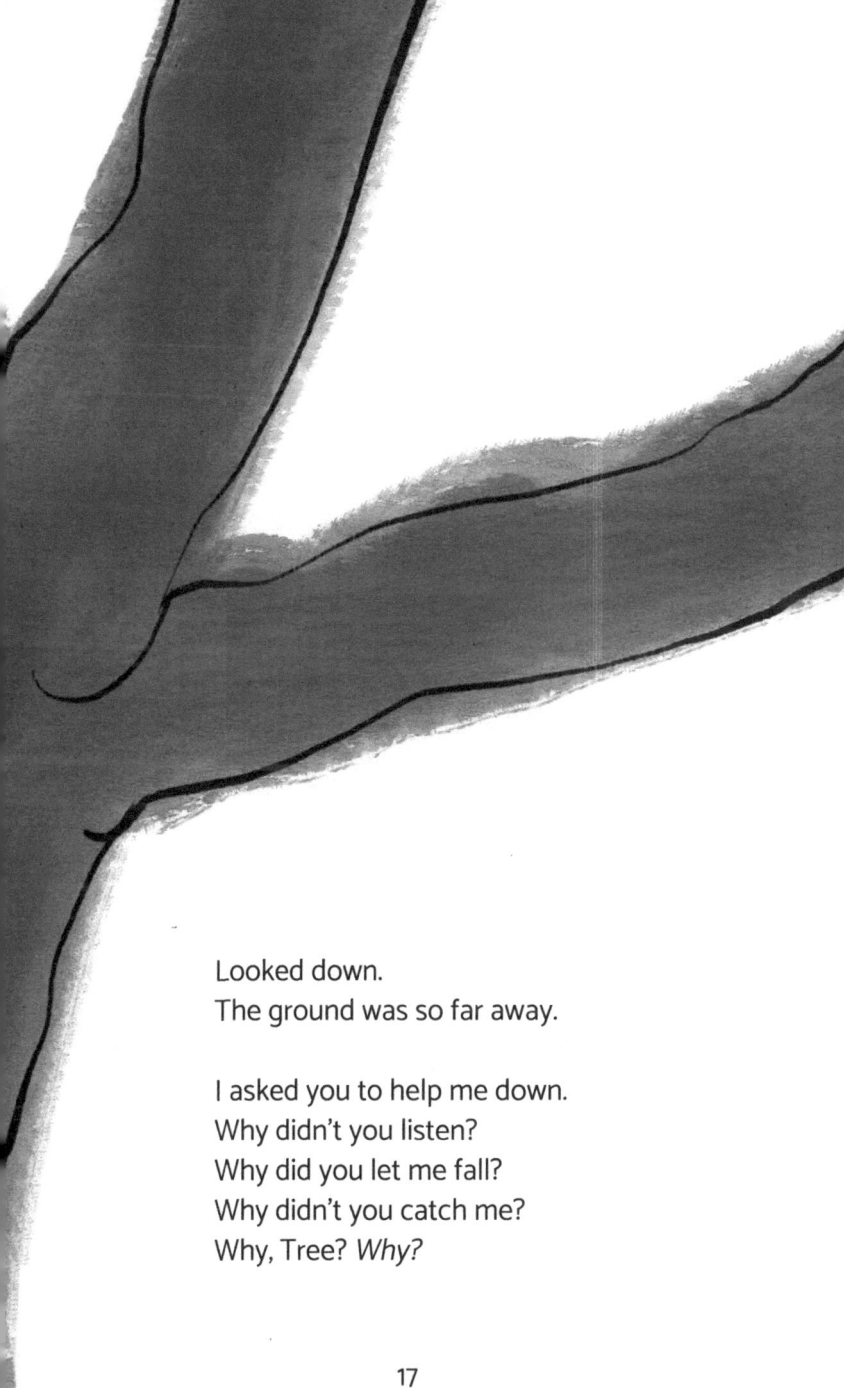

Looked down.
The ground was so far away.

I asked you to help me down.
Why didn't you listen?
Why did you let me fall?
Why didn't you catch me?
Why, Tree? *Why?*

It's Hard To Push A Wheelchair With A Tree In Your Finger

It's only a splinter Cosmo, Dad says.
It'll come out with a pair of tweezers.
It's not like you have a whole tree in there.

But Dad's wrong.
That splinter might not be the size of a tree
but it feels like the whole of you in there.
Every time I push my wheels, I only think of you.
And I want you out of my finger.

Like I want you out of the garden.
I want someone to dig up your roots,
put you on the back of a van and move you
so very far from here.

Maybe an island, or the top of Everest?
Or at the very very top of some steps and stairs,
so there's no way I could ever visit.

And then some day, I'll be able to look out the window,
see a space at the end of the garden
and forget you were ever there.

Weeping Tree

*I've cried many a leaf for branches
I've watched fall and break.*

*But there are not enough leaves
in all the woods and forests
to make the tears I wanted to shed
after I watched you fall -
out of my grasp
down to the ground.*

Everyone Tells Me What I Can't Do, Apart From Mum

Nana says, *you can't be an astronaut—*
too many ladders on a spaceship.

Brian from next door who cuts our grass, says,
you can't use a lawnmower lad, might chop
your toes off.

Ana shouts from the top of the stairs,
YOU CAN'T CATCH ME.

Funny how she always forgets we have a lift
and gasps when she sees me
beam up through the floor.

Sometimes I think the only thing I can do
is sit and think about the things I'm told I can't do.

Mum's not like that though. When I tell her I can't
tidy my room, she folds her arms
and gives me that look.

She shakes her head from side to side and says,
*If you can make your room untidy in your wheelchair
then you can definitely make it tidy in your wheelchair.*

I have no answer to that.

A Poem From Mum

Hello, Tree.
I'm Sally, Cosmo's mum.

Don't worry, I'm not here with an axe.
I just want to look and see if my little boy
left anything up there.

I don't blame you for what happened.
You're just a tree. But since the accident
it's like he left some things behind.

He's lost his smile.
He's stopped playing outside.
His football boots have gone.
So has his pride at being a big brother.
He avoids the skatepark–
he used to love whizzing
down the half pipe.
Where's his imagination that could turn
a box into a ship and your branches,
a ladder to the Moon?

I miss his sense of humour.
I miss his cheeky ways.

I used to ask him what he wanted for dinner
and he'd shout *BISCUITS!!!!*

Now he just stays quiet.
Is his love of biscuits up there?

Please help me, Tree.
Help me find the biscuits.

Bedtime

I miss my old bed.
It had a mattress, a duvet,
two pillows and a ladder.
Beds with ladders are the best.
You know I loved climbing,
and climbing into bed like a firefighter
made bedtimes *EPIC*.
Once I reached the top
I'd snuffle under the duvet.

Mum and Dad gave my old bed away.
I can't climb into bed now.
Just like I can't become a wrestler, jump
off the big diving board or ride a motorbike
through a ring of fire. One more thing
I can't do.

Instead, I slide into bed
on a board. Stunt people don't slide into bed
on a board. They probably somersault from
a moving car.

One side of the board sits on my wheelchair,
the other on my bed
        and I shuffle across.

It sounds more fun than it is.

Red Marks

At night Mum and Dad take it in turns
to check my skin for red marks.

They look at my hips, my ankles, the bony bit
of my bum that sits on my cushion.

Every time I see a doctor or a nurse,
they tell me red marks are BAD.

Worse than saying swear words,
dropping chewing gum or putting
cling film over the toilet seat.

Red marks mean pressure
and pressure can lead to sores
and sores are VERY BAD.
Sores could mean days in bed.
Now that is REALLY BAD. No more
surfing or goalkeeping if that happens.

Mum and Dad used to look through
my homework to see where the teachers
had put red marks.

Now they're too busy
looking at my skin.

I haven't done my homework in at least a week
and no-one's noticed.

What Do You Think At Night Time?

When it's dark outside, and all you can hear
is the wind in your branches, do you wish
you were planted somewhere else?
Do you wish you were a different tree
in a different garden?

Do you look down at your branches
and wish they'd stopped me falling?

If you'd been in another garden,
with another boy, on another day,
would you have let him go too?

Would he also lie in bed at night
and whisper to you on the other side
of the glass in his bedroom window?

Or were you meant to be in my garden?
Were you meant to watch me fall?

Stabilisers

It's *exactly* one year since I learnt to ride
my bike with no stabilisers.
I remember (after a bit of a wobble)
feeling as free as a squirrel.

I was peddling as fast as I could
and I turned to look at Dad.
Big mistake.
Down we went,
me and the bike.

You should've seen the gash on my knee!
But I didn't mind the blood,
I was still laughing from how amazing
it felt to be on two wheels.

I'm back on stabilisers again.
Now, I need four wheels to stop me
from toppling like a game of Jenga.

The doctor says these wheels will never come off,
I have to get used to them.

If I was to fall again and slash my knee
I still wouldn't cry if I saw blood.
Because I wouldn't be able
to feel the pain.

My Brother By Ana

Heya Tree,

Cosmo doesn't leave
footprints anymore,

he leaves two tyre tracks instead.
That's really cool.

Anyone can leave footprints,
that's so boring. YAWN.

And when I see his tyre tracks
I always know where he's been.

I like that,
it always feels like
he's near.

Biscuits

Mum keeps putting the biscuits in the Biscuit Cupboard.
The only problem is the Biscuit Cupboard is too high
for me to reach.

Jammy Dodgers, Wagon Wheels, Club bars, KitKats –
all beyond the tips of my fingers.
(The digestives can stay up there,
they're dry and boring).

The other biscuits, the good ones, are like
cats stuck in your branches.
I thought about calling the fire brigade
but I'm not sure that would go down too well.
Hello, this is the operator, what's your emergency?
Send a fire engine with ladders, I need biscuits.
They're stuck in the cupboard and can't get down.

I don't think Mum does it on purpose.
She's like me, still trying to figure this out
and sometimes she forgets and puts the biscuits
where I can't reach.

What Was It The Table Said?

I run my fingers over your rough bark
and it's like stroking the lines of an old man's face.
The green moss is a great big beard
(like the one that Dad jokes I'll never be able to
 grow).

I start to point.
First at my chest, then at you.

Me. Tree. Me. Tree. Me. Tree.
Me. Tree. Me. Tree. Me. Tree.
Me. Tree. Me. Tree. Me. Tree.

And I'm pretty sure I see you, old tree man,
nod from behind my hand.

Wrong, I call out.
Pointing again.

This tree, I say to the sky,
is the uncle of our wooden spoons.
The best friend of my bed.
This tree could be a bookcase, a shed,
a piano stool, a TV stand, a record box,
a rolling pin, a door frame,
a bird box, a fruit bowl.

So why, after all it's done,
does it get to just stand there?
Like nothing's happened.

Later, tired from shouting, I rest my head
on the dining room table,
press my ear against the wood.

And whisper,
what did you do to end up like this?

Climbing

Climb   a ladder
Climb   the stairs
Climb   into bed
Climb   a rope
Climb   a climbing frame
Climb   a hill
         a cliff
         a mountain
Climb   like the ivy
         up the side
         of Nana's house
Climb   a pole
Climb   a tree
Climb   a tree
Climb   a tree

        How   did this happen
                    to me?

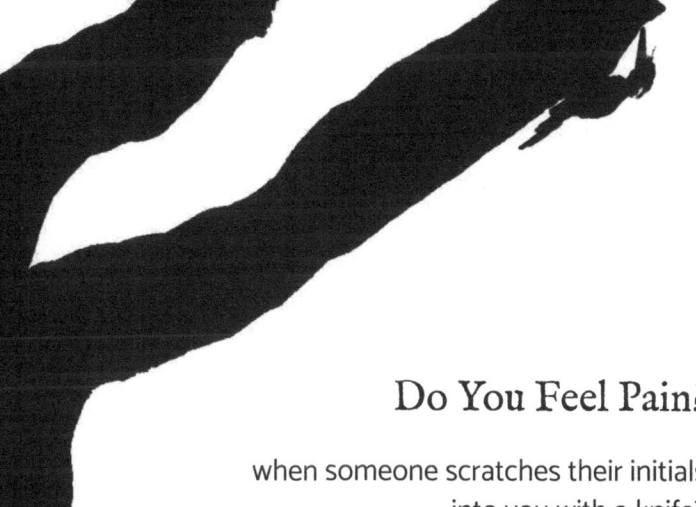

Do You Feel Pain?

when someone scratches their initials
into you with a knife?
when a squirrel scrambles up the side of you
with its scratchy claws?
when the wind blows hard against you
and snaps off your branches?
when people nail bunting to you
and fairy lights?
when each autumn your leaves fall
and the cold moves in?
when a woodpecker pecks its beak
against you over and over?
when I bash my fists against you
and ask why, why, why?

Why Does Everyone Have Something To Say?

Mum clips one end of Bertie's lead to his collar
and then the other end to my wheelchair.

Bertie doesn't care about the wheelchair.
Bertie just cares about going for a walk.

After the accident some people started
to look at me differently,
like my hair was made of jelly. It felt like they wanted
to put a spoon in my jelly hair but weren't sure
if they were allowed.

Bertie has never looked at me differently.
He sits by the door like always, his lead in his mouth
and wags his tail when he sees me,
knowing it's time for a walk.

Bertie doesn't care about the wheelchair.
Bertie just cares about going for a walk.

Mum comes with us and we head down the street,
past the camper van outside number 43 that has bricks
for wheels and has never moved. Past the 26 hairdressers,
the three nail salons, the bakers and the strange shop
that sells crystals and stinky candles.
Past the bench with the small sign
that says *For Beryl and Jeff.*

Bertie doesn't care about the wheelchair.
Bertie just cares about going for a walk.

At the park Bertie can run as fast as he likes.
The paths are smooth and if I push my chair as fast
as an F1 racing car I can keep up with his little legs.

We pass a man who chuckles and says,
Looks like he's taking you for a walk.

I stop my chair, Mum catches us up
and I unclip Bertie and pass her the lead.

Bertie doesn't care about the wheelchair.
Bertie just cares about going for a walk.

I don't want to take Bertie for a walk today.
I'd love to be invisible, just for one day.

Writing My Feelings

...it was Dad who saw it first. He was helping me get ready for bed. I knew he would see it. But I did it anyway.

My marker pen tattoos. One on each leg. In big black letters: STUPID on one leg, USELESS on the other.

Dad didn't say anything at first, he just sat down on the bed, looked at my legs and then saw the marker pen on my bedside table, on top of my football sticker book. After what felt like a whole football match, then extra time and penalties, Dad finally said something.

What's this about, pal? He patted each of my legs once with his massive hands. I wanted so much to know what that felt like. He might as well have been patting two rotten sausages.

They don't listen to me, they don't work, they don't do what I ask, I hate them, they just hang there and I have to drag them around. I want to get a saw from the shed and cut them off. So I gave myself tattoos, just like you and Mum have.

Dad looked at me and smiled. *You're a bit young for tattoos pal, besides these are only half finished.*

I watched him go over to the table and pick up the marker pen. He came back and wrote the word NOT before each of my pen tattoos. NOT STUPID, NOT USELESS.

Are you really listening, he said, *to your legs? There's still energy in there, and so much life. Your life. And you're not stupid or useless.* He reached out and gave me a hug and I breathed in his Dad smell. *We'll wash these off tomorrow,* he said...

Keep Talking Little One

Why do you trust me with your words?
You trusted me when you climbed.
And I let you down.
So many families lived in your house before you.
So many people.
Some of them came to talk.
Some told me their secrets.
Some just hugged me quietly.
And I never hurt any of them,
only you.
And yet still you come,
to read me your letters.
Please, keep talking little one.
I wish there was I way I could write back,
to say I'm sorry.

Memory Wheel

In school today I was told that trees
can live for hundreds of years.

And that for every year a tree lives,
a new growth ring forms in its trunk.

Well, I hope that the ring you grew this year
has spokes and looks like a wheel.

Because when I leave home
you'll still be growing.

When I've surfed 50-foot waves and travelled the world
you'll still be growing

When I'm old like Dad
you'll still be growing.

When I'm one hundred and six and have robots for pets
you'll still be growing.

And I hope even then, after all those years
you'll look down through your hundreds of rings,

see the one that looks like a wheel
and feel your branches shudder.

You'll see that memory wheel
and never forget me.

My Sister's Legs

There are two things I hate about Ana.

Number 1: Her left leg.
Number 2: Her right leg.

When only her head pokes out from the duvet
she's much more likeable.

When she rides on Mum's back like a rucksack
I want to be her friend again.

When she broke her ankle and had to use crutches
I was secretly happy she couldn't walk.

When I wrote on her plaster cast, *Get well soon*
I lied.

Why Cosmo Is Annoying By Ana

Why do I have to take my wellies off
when I've been outside?

Cosmo doesn't have to take his wheels off
and no-one seems to mind when he brings
mud into the house like a big messy dog.

When I leave muddy footprints on the carpet
everyone shouts
ANA TAKE YOUR WELLIES OFF!

Well, I want to leave my wellies on.
At least when I leave muddy footprints
Mum and Dad remember I'm here.

Tractor Boy

With A Bit Of Practice

It's easier than you think to push in a chair.
Some people seem confused, some are just rude.

That a boy on four wheels can be quicker
than someone on two legs, it's almost like
they're annoyed when I wheel past them.

You must be smarter than me, they say.
I couldn't do that. It's because you're young.
Kids can pick anything up.

It's not like I have a choice though, is it?
Push, be pushed, or stay stuck in my bedroom.

Don't get me wrong,
it takes some getting used to.

But so did having a sister
and she's alright I suppose.

The First Day

The first day I was in hospital,
I was flat on my back and all I could see through
the window was the tips of branches, like twig
fingers waving at me.

The first day I came home I went straight to the
windows and closed the curtains. I didn't want to look
at you, I wanted to think about anything but what
what you did to me.

The first day I went back to school, I looked out of the big
windows by my desk and saw hundreds of trees
at the edge of the school field. I couldn't see you,
but I swear they were all watching me.

Three Haiku

SURPISING PERKS
I get sausages
whenever I ask for them.
So it's not all bad.

BIRTHDAY LIST
Next year I'll be nine.
I've asked for a new helmet
so I can do tricks.

SISTER'S NICKNAME
Ana calls me Flash
'cos I'm as fast as lightning.
I feel the rain clear.

Growing

There are no more lines on the kitchen doorframe
to say how far I have grown.

Those lines stopped appearing
when I started pushing through doors.

I guess that's OK. But when I see you, I want to shout
Look, look, look how tall I am.

With every new branch
with every new leaf
with every new inch
you grow towards the sun.

And I want to shout louder to be sure you can hear me.
Look, look, look how tall I am.

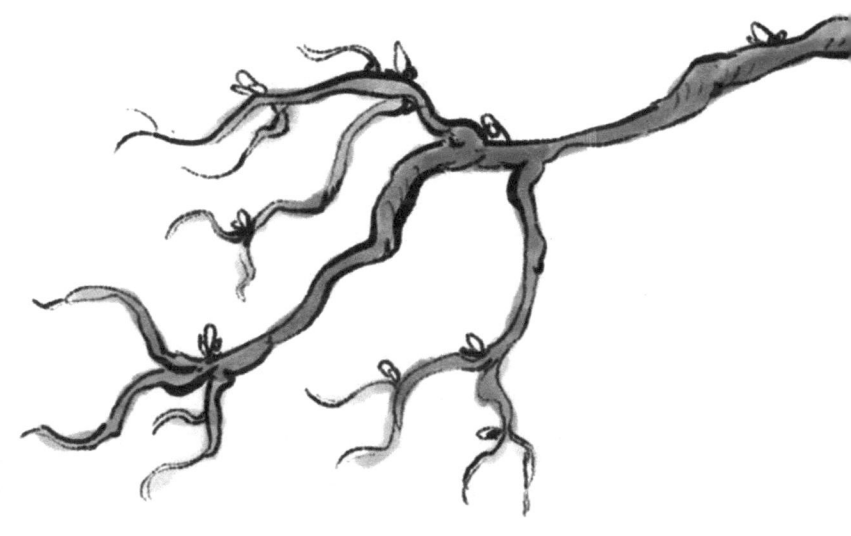

A Poem From Nana

So how does this work then?
I just say *Hello Tree* and start talking?
Bloomin' daft if you ask me.
But they say it's important, to help us
help Cosmo.

I'd have chopped you down. Chop, chop, chop.
With my bare hands if I had to.
I'd have made firewood out of you
then dug up your roots, swept away your leaves,
found all of your seeds and tossed them on the fire.
I'd have made sure there was nothing left of you.

And that still wouldn't be enough.

All that future he had in him,
what's he supposed to do now.
Stay in and watch TV, the Paralympics?
Everyone tells him he could win a medal if he tried,
sing the national anthem like a good lad.

Cosmo says he just wants to play
with his friends– I guess he won't be
climbing any trees soon.

I hope you're happy with yourself.

Choosing Things

I like choosing things.
Like when Mum asks what I want
from the ice cream van and I say,
I'll have two whippy ice creams, in a cone,
with a flake, and hundreds and thousands,
and another flake, and a bubblegum
on the top, and a spoon to eat it with,
oh and a wafer, and some
hot chocolate sauce.

(I used to like
raspberry ripple but I don't
ask for that any more.)

I like choosing where to put my books
on my bedroom shelves, or what liquids
from all the bottles in the bathroom
make the best potions, or where best
to hide Ana's favourite bear, or whether
Jammy Dodgers or Wagon Wheels
are my favourite biscuit today.

Mum and Dad have moved my trainers
from the shoe rack by the front door.
I have to put my trainers on in my bedroom now
so I don't catch my toes in my front wheels.
I caught them once, it was strange how it didn't hurt
but they bled so much it looked like raspberry ripple
all over the white bathroom tiles.

Anyway, I miss choosing what trainers to wear
when we leave the house. I just wait now,
while everyone else puts on their shoes.

I bet they wouldn't choose wheels
if they were asked.

Brave Boy

A lady in the cinema tells Mum that I'm brave
as I fill my tub with pick 'n' mix.

Mum's face looks like it does when I wheel
mud in from the garden. Sort of like a baked potato
that's been in the oven too long.

I wonder why Mum has her potato face,
is she going to tell this lady off?

I ask the lady if she thinks I'm brave because I filled
half of my tub with sour cherries
and the other half with fizzy fish.

I wonder if her cheeks are watering
from the thought of all that sour.

Mum doesn't look like a potato anymore,
instead her eyes are bulging
from holding in a giant laugh.

The strange thing is, people
tell me that I'm brave a lot.

I'm brave when ordering a hot dog at the football.
I'm brave when trying on trainers at the shoe shop.
I'm brave when throwing balls through a hoop on the pier.
I'm brave when I go with Nana to the greengrocers
to buy bananas.

No one seems to call Ana brave when she tries shoes on
and she's only five.

I know they're scared of my wheelchair
and they don't know if they could smile as much as I do
if they had to push to the shops.

But I don't smile because I'm brave,
I smile because I'm happy.

Biscuits For Dinner

Hi Tree, it's Cosmo's mum again.
Today I asked Cosmo
what he wanted for dinner.
Biscuits, he said with a cheeky smile.
We had biscuits for dinner.
We had all the biscuits,
apart from the digestives of course,
then we went and bought
some more.

I thought you'd be happy
to know that.

Cloudspotting

In the summer Dad lifts me out of my wheelchair
and places me on a mat in the garden.

From there I lie down on my back
and look at the clouds drifting by.

I stretch out my arms,
rub the grass with my fingers
and watch the candyfloss clouds play.

Clouds don't get sad,
they can crash and bang and not get hurt,
they don't need help to climb
the stairs.

They dash and fly and swirl and rush,
the wispy cirrus clouds playing hide and seek
above the grumpy cumulonimbus.

From up there, where they cuddle the aeroplanes,
do any of them stop their playtime and watch
this little boy watching them,

smiling?

Pushing

I wheel
where it's flat
where it's smooth
not down stairs
or over cobbles.
Sand is tricky,

but fun with Dad.
Bouncy castles,
not for me.
Carpet at Nana's house,
pain in the bum.
Shiny flooring
at school
and the playground,
they're both cool.
Probably good
on the ice,

but ice skates
not a chance.

Ducks

Yesterday Mum said *where's your welly?*
The ducks stole it and that's the truth.
A group of them - twenty, thirty, maybe
 a hundred
and I think a swan too.
Just how did the ducks steal your welly?
It was a good question.

Well, I pushed across the field near the river
and there they were.
Rushing as one towards me.
Like a giant bus-sized duck.

QUACK QUACK QUACK
QUACK QUACK QUACK
QUACK QUACK QUACK
I nearly did a quack in my pants!

So I took off my welly and threw it at them–
easier to wang a welly than push in the mud.
The ducks grabbed the welly and pulled it into the river.
Mum asked, *why didn't you just throw all the duck food?*
That's a good point, I thought, looking down
at the bag of duck food on my knee.

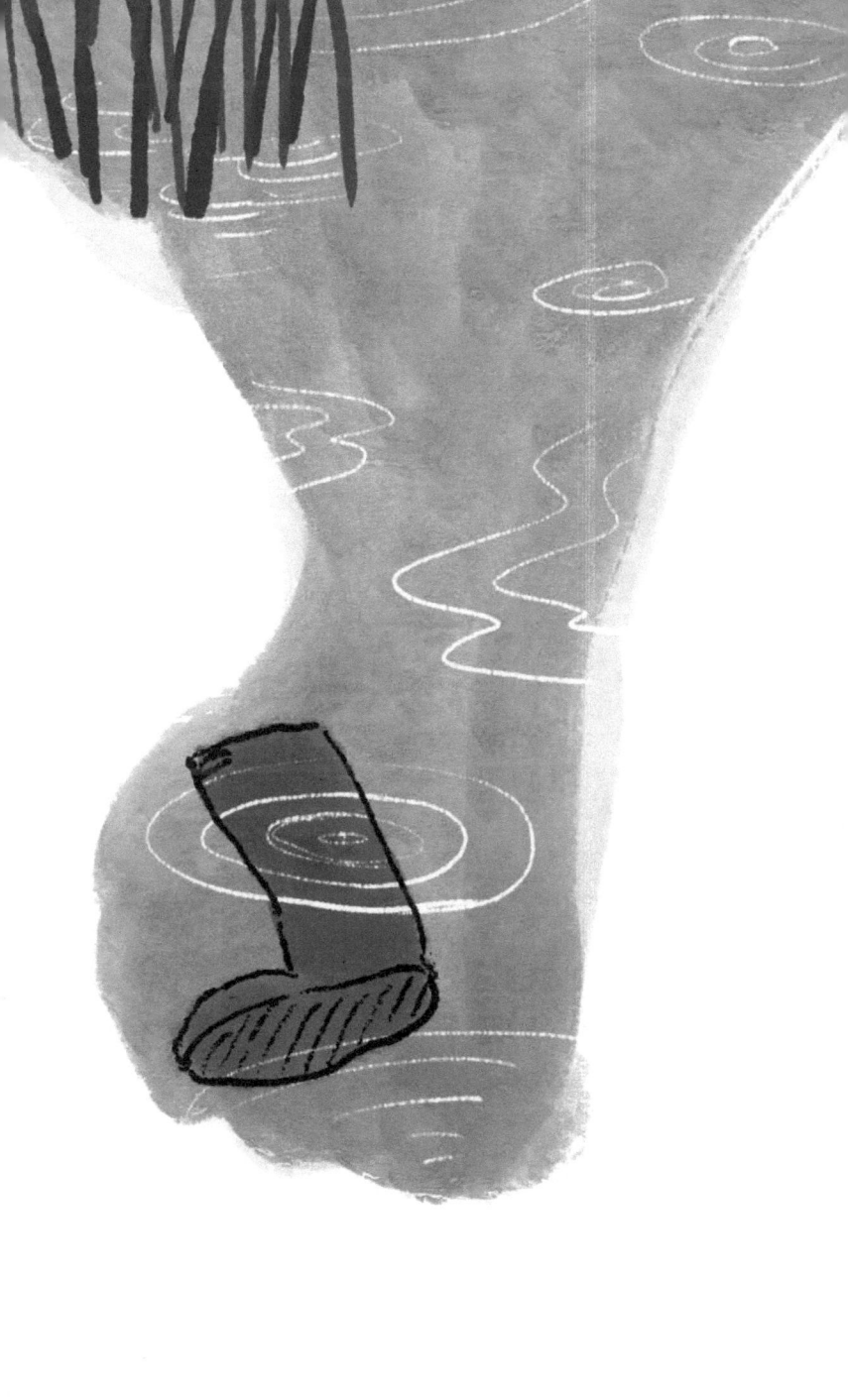

Running Away

Sometimes, I come and sit by you
at the end of the garden
because that's the last place my legs worked.

I try to imagine all the things I'd do if they worked again.
I imagine how I'd run away from home, away from you.
But I guess I wouldn't run away if my legs worked –
there'd be no need, it would all be OK.

But it's not OK.
I tried to run away last week.

I made it as far as the end of the street.
A neighbour saw me pushing on my own
and phoned Mum who came and got me.

So I push here, to the end of the garden
to look at where I last remember using my legs
and think about how stuck I feel.

Good Listener

Everyone keeps asking how I am
but what can I say?

If I say I'm sad, they say
I should be thankful I'm still here.

If I say I'm doing OK, they say
that's surprising after what I've been through.

If I say I'm angry, they say
I should've been more careful.

If I say I don't know how I am, they say
I should talk more.

But no-one wants to listen.
Apart from you.

You're the only one I can talk to.
You're a good listener for a tree.

Broken Branches

When the wind blows
        and a branch falls off,
                do other trees call you disabled?

Do you just
            grow another one?

Do the other trees
        treat you differently?
               Or maybe they see that

you're still the same tree.

My Heart Beats, I Dance

In the studio on the big
shiny floor we get ready.
First on go our disco-dance leggings.
Neon yellows, pinks, oranges.
I choose lime-jelly green.

Next, we dab on silver glitter,
get rid of shyness,
tie laces.

Our teacher claps three times
and we all move into position.
Some run, others glide.
I push.

I have two arms,
               two legs,
                             four wheels.

I come here to find
new ways to move.

Out there, where other hands
hold me back, I'm called disabled.
But who decides?
Here, when we begin to move

we're all dancers,
we're all able.

Our teacher says
'life is an improvisation'.
Here feels natural, free.
Here I tell my story.

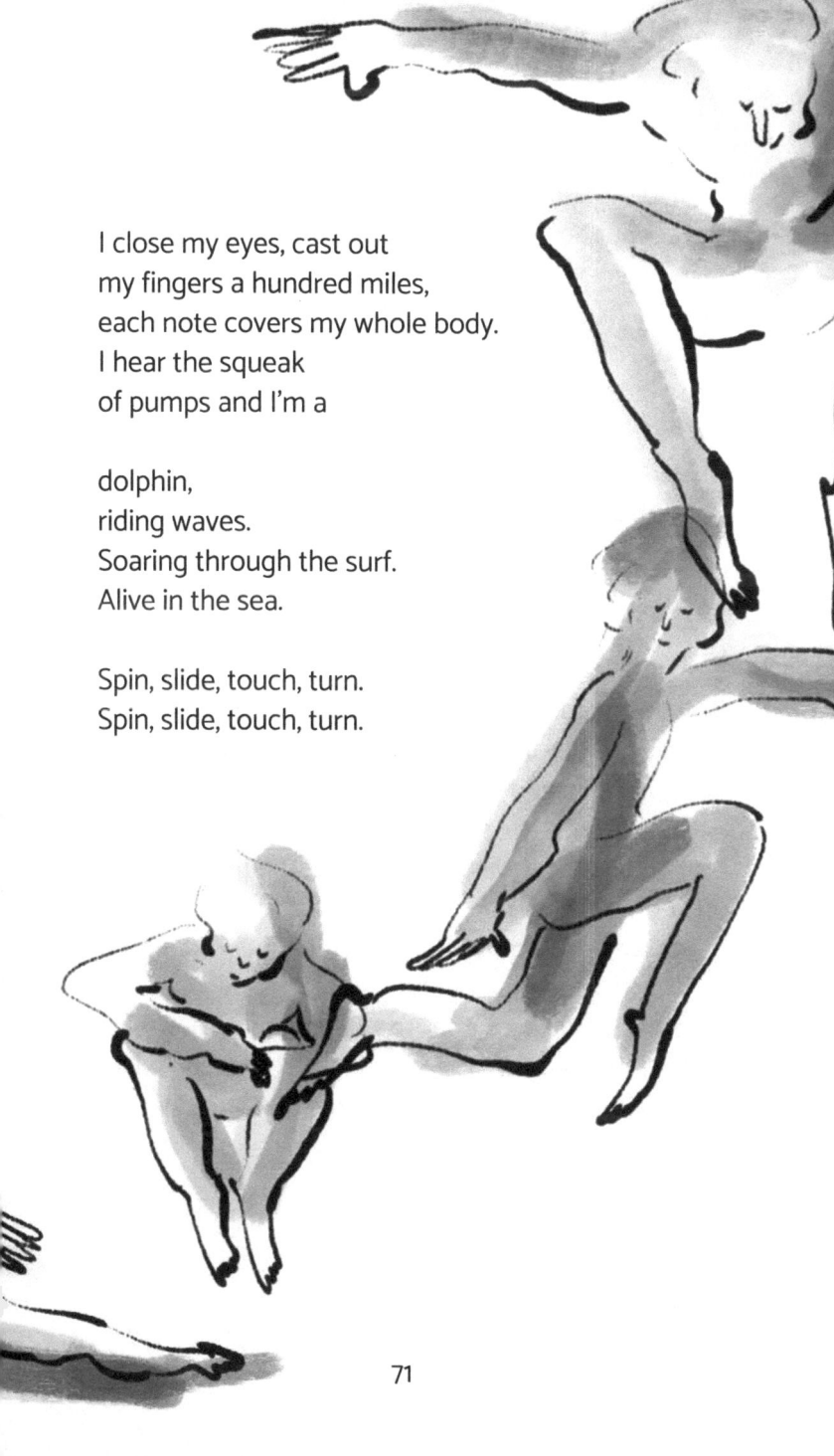

I close my eyes, cast out
my fingers a hundred miles,
each note covers my whole body.
I hear the squeak
of pumps and I'm a

dolphin,
riding waves.
Soaring through the surf.
Alive in the sea.

Spin, slide, touch, turn.
Spin, slide, touch, turn.

Running A Marathon In Custard

Every Sunday, Dad goes for a run.
He runs ten miles, to the park, round the lake,
up the hill past the benches where we sit and look
across our town, then he runs home by the bakery
and gets pastries for breakfast.

Dad says one day he'll run a marathon again
and this time he'll get a personal-best time.
I wonder what he'd get if, instead of trainers,
he had to run the race with two washing-up bowls
filled with lumpy custard strapped to his feet?

All that training he'd do ready for the race, mile
after mile around the park saying hello to Maggie
and her sausage dog every Sunday for six months.
His legs would be strong, his feet healed of blisters,
a personal-best waiting for him at the finish line.
Then – bang! – change of plan.
Two washing-up bowls. Filled with lumpy custard.

He'd watch as runner after runner jogged past him
all in their fancy trainers. He'd look at them and think
if only I had my trainers instead of custard
I'd have been unstoppable.

He'd still try though, do his best.

Sometimes I think my wheelchair is custard.
And I do my best too.

The Day Is A Bad Dream On Repeat

Imagine
pushing, pushing, pushing
all day. Every day.

No days off.
Not a single one.

After rice pudding and a huge spoon
of red jam for dessert I can't wait to
sleep sleep sleep

because in my dreams, I'm walking.
Running, skating, kicking footballs, jumping
on bouncy castles, pedalling so fast my legs
are a blur.

Then I wake up, see my wheelchair
and all I want is to be asleep again.

Sleep-Walking

I say goodnight to Mum and Dad
and I wait for them to turn the light off
and close the door.

When I know I'm alone
I scrunch my eyes shut,
wait for sleep and then
I go for a walk.

You might not see me,
putting one foot in front of the other,
striding down the street
but that doesn't mean I'm not walking.
Like, we don't see your bark lift and fall
when you breathe, because you're a tree.
But we know you're alive.

The doctors told me I would never walk again
but they don't decide my dreams. I don't even know
if I choose what I dream about because in one dream
I was playing football for Arsenal
and I definitely DO NOT support Arsenal.

A Kenning About My Wheelchair

Bottom Holder
Beach Sinker
Stair Avoider
Stare Gatherer
Leg Replacer
Conversation Starter
Shiny Stallion
Queue Jumper
Plus One
Cobble Hater
Homework Excuser
Ramp Lover
Goal Blocker
Pigeon Scatterer
Cosmo Throne

What To Do With A Dying Tree

Was the middle of Blackburn Road better
than wherever it escaped from? The tree was a mess,
leaves and branches all crushed and tangled.

It must've been scared and run away.
Did it come from a garden like ours?

I put my hand on it,
waited for it to move but
its bare branches stayed still.

It was the length of two of Dad's weight benches–
not a big tree, but still a tree.

Like you.

I couldn't bring it home.
We've only got a small garden
and you take up most of it.

I told it to remember
all the backs, the feet, the resting grandmas
that leant against it. The little boys
who climbed its branches and didn't fall.

How far would you walk
on your roots to forget us?

Huff Stop

We had to take the bus today.
I hadn't been on a bus in my wheelchair before.

The bus driver huffed because he had to
get off the bus to lower the ramp for me to get on.

The lady huffed because she had to
move her suitcases from in front of the sign that said
PLEASE GIVE PRIORITY TO WHEELCHAIRS.

The man huffed because he had to
move his six carrier bags full of shopping
so that Mum could sit down and when she did
he made a loud tutting noise.

The boy with the massive headphones huffed
because he dropped his phone and it skidded
under my chair and took ages to get it back.

The bus driver huffed again when we got to the library
and he had to get off the bus again to lower the ramp
for me to get off.

Buses are very huffy places.

Bleeding Soil

Yesterday
Mum went full baked-potato face again.
This time at me.

She asked me why I'd knocked
all the plants over in the living room.

Every single one of them was on the floor,
leaves broken, stems snapped.
Even the giant one with leaves that look like hands waving
that almost reach the ceiling.
Snapping those took some effort.
I took a run up and rammed it with my wheels.

It looked like a hurricane had burgled our house.

They deserved it. I said it was payback.
I can't push the tree over, but the tree will feel the pain
of all of these. It'll feel what I did.

Mum started to cry.
I asked her if the spilled soil looked like my blood
when I lay on the ground after I fell.

Three More Haiku

SATURDAYS AT THE SKATEPARK
I'd given up hope
that on the ramps, in my chair
I could still wipe out.

BIRTHDAY LIST
In the end I fibbed.
What I want is obvious
but you can't buy it.

SUPERMARKET
The bit by the till
is exactly my height. Yes!
That's where the treats are.

Pushing Bolder

I push my wheelchair
       and I move forwards,
       away from the past,
       away from wondering why
       my legs don't work.
I push my wheelchair
       towards another day
       where I find new ways
       to have fun.
I push my wheelchair
       and I see Mum smile
       a little more.
I push my wheelchair
       and take Bertie
       for a walk and this time
       I don't wish I could run like him
       when we let him off his lead.
I push my wheelchair
       and I feel like me again.
       Another day when I grow older.
       Another day when I grow bolder.

The Greatest Day

That's what I called yesterday.
I went surfing in the sea
on a surfboard with a seat.
Wetsuit on, I looked like a seal.

You should've seen the wave I surfed.
Ten feet tall! No, maybe a hundred!
As high as one hundred and twenty-three grizzly bears
standing on each other's shoulders
and just as angry as the wave.

I didn't mind the salt in my eye,
I was crying anyway.
I wasn't sad, I wasn't hurt.
I was free at last.
The water, a big blue surfboard
and me – grizzly bear wave tamer.

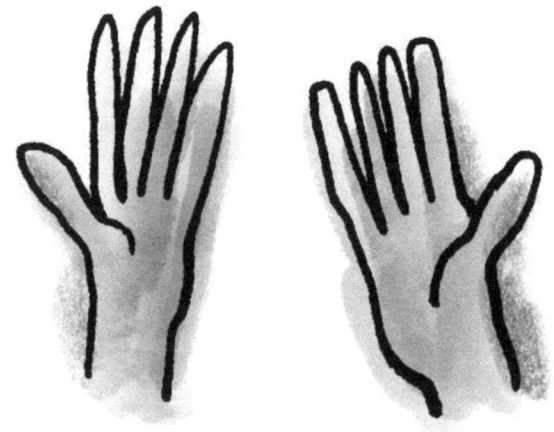

Today I'm A Tree Too

I have ten branches for fingers,
ten branches for toes,
roots that grow from my hair
right down to my wheelchair.
I sit proud on my cushion
and grow through the night
without making a sound.

Goalkeeper

Hey! Tree!
I rushed here as quick as I could
and I'm all out of breath.
I wanted to tell you.
Today at school, I played in goal
as an actual goalkeeper!
Can you believe it?
Normally, I'm scared to join in.
How could I play in goal in my wheelchair?
My friends ask every day
and I always say no, but today,
today I said yes.
I don't know why,
but I did, and I loved it!
I saved a penalty, a header,
three shots from my best friend Malcolm
and a carrier bag that got caught in the wind.
Sally scored, but she always does,
even against Taz and he's the first choice
for the school team.
I filled that goal like a donkey stuck in a cat flap.
It was brilliant, I was brilliant, today was brilliant.
See, Tree, just like you told me,
I can still be brilliant.

Be Careful With Scissors

I cut the legs off the footballers
in my magazines. SNIP SNIP SNIP.
No more kicking for them.
Legless.

I cut the legs off Ana's Duggee toy.
And Sparklebot. And her magical unicorns.
SNIP SNIP SNIP.
And the knitted dinosaur Mum made for me.
Legless.

I cut the legs off my Pikachu toy
and hid all the Lego mens' legs.
The legs of my scorpion models, SNIP SNIP SNIP.
Legless.

If I can't cut my own legs off
these will have to do.
SNIP SNIP SNIP.

If Only Trees Could Catch

I would be the tallest person in class
I would eat all the biscuits I want
I would score the winning goal at Wembley
I would not have a scar from my neck to my bum crack
I would not know how to push a wheelchair
I would ride a lion through the town centre
I would catch a ride on a rocket to the Moon
I would walk Bertie every day
I would swim across the sea and buy an ice cream in France
I would learn to fly a plane, buy a plane and fly away
I would chop down trees that can't catch
I would play frisbee in the woods
I would scare a goat, drink a Coke float, sail on a Lego boat
I would hop with my eyes closed, singing songs while eating jelly
I would probably still climb trees
I would not have met robots in hospital
I would not have to talk to a tree in the garden
I would not have had the worst year in the history of the world
I would not wish I was anybody but Cosmo

Cosmo

Last night I had a bad dream. I dreamt I was a tree
and I all I could move was my branches.
My trunk was stuck in the ground.
People came up to me and hugged me
and told me everything would be OK
and I'd get used to being a tree.
But I'm not a tree, being a tree would be
different. And I'm not different, I laugh
and whoop and dash and spin.
I'm still Cosmo. I've always been Cosmo.
I will always be
Cosmo.

Acknowledgements

A quick note of thanks to several people who have helped make this book possible. First, a huge thank you to Troika for believing in me and encouraging me to branch out into writing for children. To Martin West and Roy Johnson: many thanks for this opportunity–you have been wonderful to work with. To Shauna Darling Robertson: these poems exist in the way they do thanks to your fabulous editorial skills and your belief in the words I was putting to page.

Thank you to Jackson Lightbown for letting me borrow your story about ducks for a poem. Thanks also to The Dirigible Balloon and The Toy Press who first published some of these poems.

A huge thank you to Shih-Yu Lin for the incredible illustrations on the cover and throughout this book. I adore the way the artwork brings the poems to life. And thank you to Wendy Mach for your creative design throughout the book.

Finally, the most important thank you goes to Carly, for space to write, encouragement to imagine, and love when I don't have the strength to write my own poems to a certain tree.

About The Author

Stephen Lightbown

Stephen Lightbown grew up in Lancashire and now lives in Bristol with his wife and son. He writes extensively but not exclusively about life as a wheelchair user, and is passionate about seeing and hearing authentic voices on disability.

Stephen has appeared at events across the UK, including Shambala, WOMAD, Verve and Lyra Bristol festivals. In 2021 he wrote and performed a one-man show, *A Life With PIP*. He has two poetry collections for adults, *Only Air* (2019) and *The Last Custodian* (2021), both published by Burning Eye Books. *And I Climbed And I Climbed* is his first collection for children.

In 2020 Stephen left a long career in NHS communications and public relations to focus on his own writing and to qualify as a yoga teacher. He is also a keen surfer and in 2022 he represented England at the ISA World Para Surf Championships in California.

About The Illustrator

Shihyu Lin

Shih-Yu was born in Taipei in Taiwan and grew up in a village surrounded by mountains. He now lives in London.

Shih-Yu graduated from Cambridge School of Art's MA in children's book illustration and says 'I've never stopped drawing since'.

His debut picture book, *An Ordinary Story*, was published by Troika in 2018. More recently, he illustrated Coral Rumble's acclaimed poetry collection, *Things That Should be in a Poem* (Troika, 2022).

troika

The home of great children's books

Troika is a small independent children's book publisher. We're based in the UK.

www.troikabooks.com

Follow us on social media

 @TroikaBooks

 @TroikaBooks